THE LITTLE BOOK OF
PUPPY
TIPS

ANDREW LANGLEY

First published in Great Britain in 2007 by
Absolute Press
Scarborough House, 29 James Street West
Bath BA1 2BT, England
Phone 44 (0) 1225 316013 **Fax** 44 (0) 1225 445836
E-mail info@absolutepress.co.uk
Web www.absolutepress.co.uk

A catalogue record of this book is available
from the British Library

ISBN 13: 9781904573623

Printed and bound in Italy by Legoprint

THE LITTLE BOOK OF
PUPPY
TIPS

ANDREW LANGLEY

'There is no faith which has never yet been broken, except that of a truly faithful dog'

Konrad Lorenz (1903–1989)

You want to buy a puppy? Well,

think long and hard about it first.

Puppies grow up into dogs, and dogs can live for fifteen years or more. You will have to look after them, feed them and exercise them all

that time. **A dog is a commitment, not a toy.**

Be sure to find out how big your pup is going to be.

A little puppy may look cute and cuddly, but it may grow up into a giant. Unless you have a big house and garden, stick to medium or small breeds.

Take a close look at the parents (if available),

and see what your puppy will turn into.
They will give you clues about its eventual size,
as well as its temperament and general health.

How do you choose a puppy?

Being confronted with a wrestling mass of new-born pups is not the easiest selection process. But it all depends what you want. Confident, adventurous puppies will clamber all over you. Quieter, more timid types will stay away and look bashful.

Work out your budget beforehand.

Dogs cost money – in vets' bills, equipment, kennels, pet insurance and food. And big dogs eat a lot more than little ones.

Deciding on the Sex: Female.

A bitch will be more serene and easier to train than a male dog (though there are – of course – exceptions). But she will probably demand more of your attention, and can get broody (and snappy) at times if not neutered.

Deciding on the Sex: Male.

Male dogs, like their human counterparts, are usually messier, clumsier and more energetic than females. This also means that they may be more aggressive with other dogs.

Puppies need your time and attention.

Young or old, dogs love company. They easily grow bored on their own, and this can lead to distress and sometimes destructive behaviour. If you get a puppy, be prepared to spend most of every day with it.

Inspect your puppy closely before choosing.

It should have clear, bright eyes, a healthy coat, and clean ears and tail. Steer clear of pups who are skinny or pot-bellied (a sign of worms).

Get your dog neutered.

This saves them – and you – a lot of grief. Unneutered males wander in search of romance, and unneutered females come into season about twice a year. A simple operation stops this, and prevents unwanted litters. Ask your vet about the best age for getting this done.

Always provide plenty of water.

Modern 'complete' foods are sometimes very dry, so dogs need access to a dependable supply of water. Rinse out the bowl regularly, and refill it with fresh water.

Your Puppy's Bed No.1: What Kind?

Something small and temporary will do at first – after all, the pup will soon grow out of it. And, of course, he or she will probably chew chunks out of it. So buy a rigid plastic dog basket or simply cut the front off a cardboard box. Line with a washable bean bag or blanket.

If you're hankering after a pure-bred puppy,

be aware of the pluses and minuses. The biggest plus is that you know what the adult dog will be like (its parents). The biggest minus is that pure-breds are more likely to inherit medical problems (because of the limited gene pool).

Feed bowls and water bowls must be tough and stable.

Puppies will chew them, fall over them and push them about. Buy heavy metal or ceramic bowls which are harder to shift and cannot be tipped over.

Put a collar on your puppy as soon as you get it home.

Buckle it just tight enough for you to fit two fingers easily underneath. The puppy may scratch at it or rub its neck on the floor, but will soon get used to the idea. Buy a light collar at first – the pup will soon grow out of it.

The magic of mongrels lies in the surprise element.

You can never be quite sure how your puppy will turn out (even if you can identify the parents). However, mongrels tend to be healthier than pure-bred dogs because of their mixed stock.

A mongrel pup is cheaper to buy than a pure-bred one.

The smarter and purer the breed, the more expensive it is likely to be. A scruffy cross-breed will cost much less to purchase – though the same to maintain.

Your Puppy's Bed No.2: Where?

Site the bed away from draughts and other disturbances. Puppies will often make the decision for you, and favour a particularly warm and congenial spot. Recognize this, and move the bed there.

Just like humans,

dogs need their own space to retire to. This is usually

their bed. Everyone should respect their privacy and think twice before disturbing them. The old dictum 'let sleeping dogs lie' is a very sensible one.

Always remember that dogs are pack animals.

And a pack needs a dominant leader. That means you! You have to be the boss from the very beginning, otherwise the dog will get ideas above its station. It may even try to dominate you and your family – with disastrous results.

You set the agenda. The puppy doesn't.

So be strong in the face of all attempts at bullying or wheedling you into unscheduled feeds or walks. Make sure the puppy knows that you decide when these things happen (except, of course, for calls of nature).

Getting your pup to sleep

on the first night at home may be difficult

(for both of you). **Be firm but gentle.** Take the puppy outside to relieve itself, then put it to bed. Ignore any pitiful whining and howling, and just leave it alone. It will soon learn the routine of settling down for the night.

Air the pup's bedding every day.

This means taking it outside and giving it a good shake to get rid of hairs, bits of mud and other unmentionables.

Wash the bedding every fortnight.

Your Puppy's Bed No.3: In A Cage?

Locking your dog in a wire cage may seem a bit of a harsh measure. Dogs don't see it that way. Leave the door open at first, and they soon get used to the cage. It becomes their nest and refuge, and they will go in quite happily.

Make sure your puppy knows his or her place.

That means the floor or the cage. Chairs, sofas and beds should be right out, as the puppy will deposit hairs, mud and (possibly) fleas. Start with this firm rule, and you won't have any trouble.

Be consistent in your treatment and attitudes.

Puppies like to feel secure, and unusual behaviour distresses them. They must be able to rely on you as a still point in an unfamiliar world.

Puppies need plenty of toys.

Like babies, they delight in chewing things – from books to table legs. Preserve your furniture and give them rubber bones and rings, leather chews or even old plastic bottles. Toys which squeak or rattle or crunch provide even more fun.

Don't lose your puppy.

Get it chipped

by having a microchip tag implanted (it takes seconds and doesn't hurt). The code can then be read by vets or the RSPCA.

And clip a name tag to the puppy's collar, complete with name, address and phone number.

Let's face it – **your puppy will mess on the carpet at least once.**

Try to make sure this doesn't happen too often.

Anticipate your pet's needs.

As soon as it wakes up, and after feed and exercise, it will need to relieve itself. Take it calmly outside and watch till the business is complete.

Cats and dogs do mix.

Unlike cartoon stereotypes, puppies and cats usually become friends.

Introduce them gently.

The puppy will probably be confused at first (what is this creature?) but, if the cat runs off, it may give chase. Separate the two calmly and try again later. They'll soon get used to each other.

Ever been on a lead? No? Then imagine how strange it must feel for a puppy.

Take time to accustom it to walking on a lead.
Put the lead on for a few minutes and take the puppy round the garden. Discourage it from pulling with a sharp tug (though it is far better to have taught it to 'heel' first – *see Tip No.36*).

Look out for tell-tale signs of imminent messing.

The pup will hurry about purposefully, usually in circles and usually sniffing at the floor. This means that something is bursting for release. You'll soon get to recognize this behaviour, and be ready to act accordingly.

The first and most important command is 'come'.

Happily, this is also an easy one to teach. Hold out a biscuit and say the command word (it can be 'here' or 'come', or simply a whistle). The puppy will naturally head for the food. Repeat the command as it approaches, and reward it with the treat.

Keep the teaching sessions brief.

A puppy has a short attention span, and easily gets tired. Start off with a couple of minutes, concentrating on a single command. Build up to no longer than five minutes.

Clean peed-on carpet as swiftly and thoroughly as possible.

Dog urine leaves two weighty legacies – stain and smell (which attracts other dogs). Blot up the moisture with a cloth, then soak the area with soda water. Dab with well diluted biological laundry liquid (to eat up the pong) and leave to dry.

Teaching your pup to stay at 'heel' is a crucial lesson.

It means you can trust it to stick near you whatever the situation. Hold your right hand down with a treat enclosed, and command the puppy to 'heel'. Reward with the treat. Graduate to walking with the puppy at heel, keeping it always on the same side and just behind you.

Puppies need regular meals.

Feed four times a day at first, then cut down to two. Find a routine that suits you both and stick to it. Resist the temptation to feed your puppy between meals (except for training treats). Even puppies get overweight.

Human mealtimes are sacrosanct. They have

nothing to do with dogs. When you are about to eat, send the puppy to its bed or cage – and make sure it stays there. Make a firm family rule not to feed dogs from the table. It's unhygienic and gets them into bad habits.

The Pavlov's Puppy Effect.

Have a key word to repeat when you take your puppy out to relieve itself.

Any short, reassuring phrase or word will do (even 'good boy'). Once the pup gets used to the sound, it will act as a psychological trigger. Restricted use is advisable.

Buy your puppy the best food you can afford.

Growing pups need large amounts of protein, fats and carbohydrates, but in an easily digestible form. That means meat (in some form) plus cereals and oils. Fresh food is great, but 'complete' prepared feeds are excellent too. Remember to keep the water bowl topped up.

Give a dog a bone?

Well – within strict limits. A good hard, uncooked bone (beef is much the best) provides hours of chewing, which is good for gums and teeth. Avoid anything else, including lamb, pork and poultry, which can splinter and cause horrible internal damage.

Exercise is a dog's greatest joy.

It keeps them fit, gives them a chance to play, and brings them into contact with exciting new smells, sights and sounds. Take your puppy out for a good

walk at least twice a day.

Until its bones develop fully, limit the distance to about one mile. After that – as far as you can.

Keep your puppy **away from other dogs until its vaccinations have taken effect.** This should take about three months (but check with your vet). Allow them to mix too early, and they risk catching a disease.

Make sure your garden is puppy-proof.

Check fences and hedges for pup-sized holes.
Have a gate that can be properly closed.
And remember that puppies will chew anything
– from power cables and garden hoses to
weedkiller bottles and slug pellets. Keep them
well out of reach.

Take time to observe your puppy.

Watch the way it moves and reacts to things.

Know all about its behaviour patterns.

In this way, you can quickly spot anything out of the ordinary – a dry nose (high temperature?), off its food (stomach upset?), a limp (thorn in the paw?), and so on.

Another (quite) easy lesson:

teaching your puppy to sit.

Hold the collar with one hand and give the command 'sit'. At the same time, press gently down with your other hand on the pup's rear end. It should sit. Reward it with a treat.
After a few lessons, the command alone should be enough.

Most dogs love car trips.
Take a few trial spins to get them used to it,

and to make sure they don't get car sick.
On long journeys, stop every couple of hours for
water and exercise. Make sure there's plenty of
ventilation. And never leave your pup in a hot car
– even for a few minutes.

Puppies need protection against parasites.

At some time or other, every dog picks up worms, fleas or some other body invader. So dose them regularly with the requisite medicines from your vet. Puppies should be treated against roundworm every three months until they are one year old.

Give your puppy a regular brush

(this is especially important for the hairier varieties). At least once a week, go all over with a brush or comb. While you're at it, inspect the ears and check for ticks, bumps and other problems. Almost all puppies adore the whole ceremony of grooming.

Love your puppy.

Puppies thrive on attention and affection – and they'll give it back to you in spades. Make their lives fun, with a secure home, lots of outdoor exercise and regular opportunities to socialize with other dogs and humans. Best of all – have two puppies!

Andrew Langley

Andrew Langley is a writer with a long experience of looking after dogs and cats. He bought his first puppy when he was still a teenager at school. Other animals which have featured in his life include sheep, chickens, geese, pigeons and honeybees. A spell on a Welsh hill farm later introduced him to beef cattle. He now lives in Wiltshire and Aveyron with his wife, two dogs and a cat.

THE LITTLE BOOK OF
BARBECUE TIPS
ANDREW LANGLEY

THE LITTLE BOOK OF
BEER TIPS
ANDREW LANGLEY

THE LITTLE BOOK OF
HERB TIPS
WILLIAM FORTT

THE LITTLE BOOK OF
POKER TIPS

THE LITTLE BOOK OF
GARDENING TIPS
WILLIAM FORTT

THE LITTLE BOOK OF
CHEFS' TIPS
RICHARD MAGGS

THE LITTLE BOOK OF
SPICE TIPS
ANDREW LANGLEY

THE LITTLE BOOK OF
GOLF TIPS
PETER FRENCH

THE LITTLE BOOK OF
TIPS SERIES

THE LITTLE BOOK OF
CHEESE
TIPS
ANDREW LANGLEY

THE LITTLE BOOK OF
WINE
TIPS
ANDREW LANGLEY

THE LITTLE BOOK OF
AGA
TIPS²
RICHARD MAGGS

THE LITTLE BOOK OF
COFFEE
TIPS
ANDREW LANGLEY

THE LITTLE BOOK OF
TEA
TIPS
ANDREW LANGLEY

THE LITTLE BOOK OF
AGA
TIPS³
RICHARD MAGGS

THE LITTLE BOOK OF
AGA
TIPS
RICHARD MAGGS

THE LITTLE BOOK OF
CHRISTMAS
AGA
TIPS
RICHARD MAGGS

THE LITTLE BOOK OF
RAYBURN
TIPS
RICHARD MAGGS

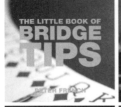

THE LITTLE BOOK OF
BRIDGE
TIPS

PETER FRENCH

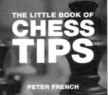

THE LITTLE BOOK OF
CHESS
TIPS

PETER FRENCH

THE LITTLE BOOK OF
FISHING
TIPS

MICHAEL DEVENISH

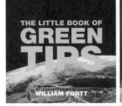

THE LITTLE BOOK OF
GREEN
TIPS

WILLIAM FORTT

THE LITTLE BOOK OF
KITTEN
TIPS

ANDREW LANGLEY

MARMITE

PAUL HARTLEY
THE LITTLE BOOK OF
MARMITE
TIPS

THE LITTLE BOOK OF
PUPPY
TIPS

ANDREW LANGLEY

THE LITTLE BOOK OF
WHISKY
TIPS

ANDREW LANGLEY

THE LITTLE BOOK OF
TRAVEL
TIPS

MEGAN DEVENISH

Little Books of Tips from Absolute Press

Tea Tips
Wine Tips
Cheese Tips
Coffee Tips
Herb Tips
Gardening Tips
Barbecue Tips
Chefs' Tips
Spice Tips
Beer Tips
Poker Tips

Golf Tips
Aga Tips
Aga Tips 2
Aga Tips 3
Christmas Aga Tips
Rayburn Tips
Puppy Tips
Kitten Tips

**All titles: £2.99 /
112 pages**

**Forthcoming
Titles:**

Travel Tips
Fishing Tips
Marmite Tips
Green Tips
Whisky Tips
Bridge Tips
Chess Tips